↑

First Figure

MICHAEL PALMER

NORTH POINT PRESS · SAN FRANCISCO · 1984

Some of these poems appeared in the following magazines:
Acts, African Golfer, Bluefish, Boxcar, Conjunctions, Ham-bone, Ironwood, the *LA Weekly, Moving Letters, Ninth Dec-ade,* the *Noe Valley Voice, Scripsi, Smithereens, Sulphur, This,* and *Writing.*

A few have been included in *Golden Gate Watershed: Nineteen American Poets,* edited by Philip Dow and pub-lished by Harcourt, Brace, Jovanovich (1984).

"Idem 1–4", directed by Eric Bowersfels, was produced for radio by KQED-FM, San Francisco.

"Echo" appeared in Ron Silliman's *In the American Tree,* National Poetry Foundation.

Contents

Niemandes Stimme, wieder.
Paul Celan

First Figure

Dearest Reader

He painted the mountain over and over again
from his place in the cave, agape
at the light, its absence, the mantled
skull with blue-tinted hollows, wren-
like bird plucking berries from the fire
her hair alight and so on
lemon grass in cafe in clear glass.
Dearest reader there were trees
formed of wire, broad entryways
beneath balconies beneath spires
youthful head come to rest in meadow
beside bend in gravel road, still
body of milky liquid
her hair alight and so on
successive halls, flowered carpets and doors
or the photograph of nothing but pigeons
and grackles by the shadow of a fountain.

Prelude

The limit of the song is this
prelude to a journey to
the outer islands, the generative
sentence, waltz project, forms,
qualities, suns, moons, rings,
an inside-outside then
an outside-inside shaped
with her colored clays. The days
yet propose themselves
as self-evident, everything there
everything here
and you are reading
in a way natural to theatre
a set of instructions
that alters itself automatically
as you proceed west
from death to friendliness, the two
topics upon which you are allowed
to meditate
under the first broad drops
of rain. The planes
will be piloted by ancestors
who have come back to life.
Why the delay.

Lies of the Poem

We welcomed the breeze
could not escape it

The face is turned to an idea
We will never be friends until it's done

His words are over
The false ceiling here

emits a remarkable light
The music is so-so

Were you named for the painting
of the moth of gold

or the stain on the pillow
The face is burned by an idea

cannot escape it
cannot escape or retain it

The body tends to disappear
beneath the wrapping

The ink dries
across a period of years

in which fires occur
at the midpoint between the eyebrows

La-la-la is the germ of sadness
said the speaker in sneakers

Sound decays
and then there is the story

and then the features are erased
The addition of one more chair

and the arrangement is complete
Here another festival

to which no one is invited
and where expectation plays no part

Voice and Address

You are the owner of one complete thought

Its sons and daughters
march toward the capital

There are growing apprehensions to the south

It is ringed about
by enclaves of those who have escaped

You would like to live somewhere else

away from the exaggerated music
in a new, exaggerated shirt

a place where colored stones have no value

This hill is temporary
but convenient for lunch

Does she mean that the afternoon should pass

in such a manner
not exactly rapidly

and with a studied inattention

He has lost his new car
of which you were, once,

a willing prisoner

a blister in your palm
identical with the sky's bowl

reflected in the empty sentence

whose glare we have completely shed
ignoring its freshness

The message has been sent

across the lesser fractures in the glass
where the listeners are expendable

The heart is thus flexible

now straight now slightly bent
and yesterday was the day for watching it

from the shadow of its curious house

Your photo has appeared
an island of calm

in a sea of priapic doubt

You are the keeper of one secret thought
the rose and its thorn no longer stand for

You would like to live somewhere

but this is not permitted
You may not even think of it

lest the thinking appear as words

and the words as things
arriving in competing waves

from the ruins of that place

Lens

I failed to draw a map and you followed it perfectly
because the word for 'cannot' inscribes itself here
to define an atmosphere of absolute trust
which both fastens and unfastens us.

The branches of the pine drooped heavily
in the moist air and this was pleasant
though at times it felt a little unpleasant
that he couldn't balance on his head

where the water trickled down the rocks.
So everything seemed small, even the problem
of whether to buy a new car
or to add a new gadget to the old car

to maintain pride of place on the block. He appears
to have seen the black pubic hair and the vagina
of a woman who squatted there to piss,
the gypsy nurse perhaps

who dealt in magic
holding the infant up with both hands.
The mist would first blur the forest's outline
then half reveal the huge limbs of the trees

or the bedside clock ticking, a red
and a white rose fastened to her breast.
She had sunk into a corner. He told
how gazing at a mountain pool

had once induced a kind of waking sleep
which led to other things.
("I am the lover in the sense of dust"
were his exact words, spoken softly.)

The child was crying out and bleeding.
Indifferently he moved on—the way
did not matter, up or down,
a few steps should be enough.

(Overheard at the)
Mayakovsky Station

"I am not that one who once spoke with you
clockwise from the pages of a voice or room
nor am I three stars in the mad queen's belt

nor snow all day, buried, nor the directive
to an hour
in N. Y.-Leningrad when the tourists board

and look down and you do the same
nor the defective hour so named.
I am concerned with this alcohol of approaching smoke

this shed for slow walkers and visitors
where return is not the intent
though they often tell of it

and of the 'having outlived'
which is the evident reason for it,
such words their gracious mistakes for things

where things are the mistake
that is trying to be made
by one who never resembled me."

French for April Fool's

I
I will name it anything I will name you this
and it rains bright stones as you say this

Each of us will call it Egypt
because of the wind

Sarah tripped and fell and spelled nest
and the wind is to blame for this

The wind has gathered a sequence of things as pure facts
Are we to become three as in three less

Is that I or me in a hat
Is that he or she in a word

Is it still early
among such stones

Is it called morning
thus to lie in a slow-drying pool

Once I could not speak of it
Now I am unable to

Truth to tell it was blood spurting from his cock
With her one good eye she would watch

They have lived long enough not to know
What flowers otherwise did we see

These are spirals
though they close at the top

Such answers varied moment by moment
mirroring the weather itself

It is a red landscape
he wondered wonderingly

I find myself here
equivalent to glass

Yet time is to be spent identifying things
This is shouting, this powdered milk

Then it is full of love and will dissolve
Then there are gestures so erected

Then shells or shelves
Then nods or knocks

A statement will be built as if to be said
"Here anything . . ."

It is an architecture
It is a stone step without question

He pulled a gun on the waiter
the young one who had poisoned him

It is a real landscape
they have invented

Truth to tell it was mud
disguised as thoughts to come

Now they are back in the park
the two who have not met before

It is a recent landscape
and the sentence is impossible

Light light murmured the dun horse
from a shaded patch covered with forget-me-nots

It is a questionable first step
impossible to correct

Voice voice cried the dumb horse
The pen trembled and began to write

strange figures on the face of night
Unread they held the answer to our plight

2
Once I could not tell of it
and now I cannot speak at all

So the cloth sticks to you there

A revolution in sportswear has occurred

So it is the park at dusk

Beer is often consumed in the dance world

The woman leans against the table painted yellow

Here it remains cold until morning

In a remote corner I am painting

Another night we slept in a yew tree

The leaf's color results from a disease

(We are speaking of murder not disease)

The bleached shirt waves

I have no crystals for you only a frame

The orange peel, a closed spiral, lies on the plate

It is the park coated with dust

He kept his mistakes beside the bed

His description was careful, even reticent

In a remote corner I am waiting

She removed her clothes as well as herself

He saw inmixing blood

(I is meant by an horizon)

Lightly the choices fell

Here it is a park

3
They have agreed to wait

We had agreed to wait for the rains

They have agreed to wait for the rains to end

I will try the blue mask on

They will remember nothing from before

I will juggle limes from the garden and sing as I'm juggling

The limes will burst where they fall

Their scent will remain after the event is forgotten

Their scent will remain after the room has dissolved

I will recall everything as it was and tell it so

Enough wind or mud to carry us away

Enough lions and monkeys to speak in our place

Enough shadow trains vanishing

Enough soldiers to keep simple order

Enough dead on the sofa enjoying the music

Enough others to serve them with easy grace

Enough *pyramids*, *heart-swings* and *valid coins of happiness*

Enough *veins full of being*

Enough maternal tones interrupting at night

These tremolos have been substituted for writing

By playing very fast the music remains in place

The fixed arc is designed to erase

What should we do in the coming white days

No Page (Unturned)

From the speaker's place of speech there's nothing
a headless man, woman or dog
at the foot of the cliff perhaps
or the assignment: to describe the sea

as best you can, the sound of the drip
then return to where it began
amid the errors and incomprehension
of conversation, thinking to tell a song

or sing a story where only sleep
is called for. How many died
in that particular December storm
or worse, turned blue and were revived

with the decorative parts missing
thus lending resonance to the story
already rejected. Revolution and gardenias
and the required film of rain

upon the plane of glass before the speaker's face
confuse the detective but please the audience
who have remained patiently in their seats since
last year's performance, refusing to become speakers themselves.

The Night Sky

A chair grows from the floor
now that the age
of classical sculpture is over.

The train starts but we are still
here, partaking
of those final moments of sleep

before sleep resumes. It shows
in the photograph
a walled city or wooden ship

the eyelids glued together
the rows of passengers content
with the absence of movement.

"Music" by David Hume

You are there because it surrounds you
It has the appearance of air

except that blue
is missing (we

have no word for it here)
from the agreement

A bit of dust on each object

They will wait until

Only the most normal dreams include everything
as events in the story

the eyes shuttling helplessly
by the morning of the fifty-fourth day

All those words we once used for things but have now discarded in order to come to know things. There in the mountains I discovered the last tree or the letter A. What it said to me was brief, "I am surrounded by the uselessness of blue falling away on all sides into fields of bitter wormwood, all-heal and centaury. If you crush one of these herbs between your fingers the scent will cling to your hand but its particles will be quite invisible. This is a language you cannot understand." Dismantling the beams of the letter tree I carried them one by one down the slope to our house and added them to the fire. Later over the coals we grilled red mullets flavored with oil, pepper, salt and wild oregano.

Poem in Two Parts

and I arrived there with closed eyes
prepared for a music in no way real, on–
off of the light, an alphabet
of forms against the hotel walls,
harbor with ships on their sides
and the taxis and ribbed water towers . . .
fearing nothing, protected by these flowers . . .

She steps down, attended
by her four rodent assistants, "grasps
at the air." The child
is unhappy and breaks things
then things break him. We share
an illness the friend said. He pressed
the accelerator and off came his head.

The Theory of the Flower

I will read a few of these to see if they exist
(We will translate logos as logos)

He swam in the rock
I am here from a distance

"Now kiss her cunt"
"Now take his cock in your hand"

The film is of a night garden
There is nothing meaningful about the text

There is nothing meaningful about a text
She

brushed away the sand
She brushed away the hand

This is Paradise, an unpunctuated book
and this a sequence of laws

in which the night sky is lost
and the flower of theory is a black spot

upon the foxglove
(These words have all been paid for)

He turns then to shade his eyes from the sun
She edges closer to the fallen log

This is Paradise, a mildewed book
left too long in the house

Now say the words you had meant to
Now say the words such words mean

The car is white but does not run
It fits in a pocket

He slept inside the rock,
a flower that was almost blue

Such is order
which exenterates itself

The islands will be a grave for their children
after they are done

You may use the paper with my name on it
to say whatever you want

I promise not to be so boring next time
never again to laugh and weep so much

which is how spring comes
to the measured center of the eye

The mind is made up
but you forget who it was first spoke

The mind is made up
and then and then

This is the paradise of emptiness
and this the blank picture in a book

I've looked over the photographs and they all are of you
just as we'd been warned

How strange
The winged figure in tuxedo is bending from the waist

The metalion addresses the mirror
and the music of the shattered window

falls unheard past the window below
How strange

but not so strange as speech
mistaken for a book

The phrase "for a moment" is popular in the world
yet not really meant to be said

That is the third or the fourth world
where you can step into a tremor with your tongue

I do not drink of it myself
but intend a different liquid

clear as the glass in which it's held,
the theory of the flower and so on

or the counter-terror of this valley
the fog gradually fills

just as we've been warned
It isn't true but must be believed

and the leaves of the sound of such belief
form a paradise

(pronounced otherwise)
from which we fall toward a window

Idem 1

(for two voices)

Let's see, how could you describe this to a listener? How can I describe this to our listeners? My head is in a steel vise I have been on a long voyage—a sea voyage—I have been travelling, sailing in a white ship, the weather is perfect surface of the water calm I am a woman or man over seven feet tall emerald green in color, malachite blue actually, tourmaline, carnelian, opal, I have been on a long voyage . . .

. . . while I have been open to desire.

Yes, while you have been open to desire, which is also blue.

I have been open to desire . . .

. . . which is like a storm or a small room . . .

. . . while you have been on a voyage, a sea voyage. You spoke of a white ship.

I did?

Yes, a white ship with twin masts. It sat in the water like a smile.

Oh right—like a smile, a white ship, gulls the first sign of land, then driftwood and kelp, then a harbor opens out before us in a perfect half-circle the water like they say clear as glass. She swung to her anchor without a flutter of the sails and was at rest. I have been travelling.

You have been at sea in a white ship with your head in a steel vise.

Exactly correct . . .

. . . while I have been open to desire, my skin an attractive shade of blue, my voice calmly assertive. How can I describe this to a listener. The room is airy and bright, a bit cold in winter, there is a washstand with porcelain pitcher and bowl, a metal cot and a wood-burning stove that rarely works. I have a fine view of the river beyond the terracotta roofs. I assume it's understood that all of this is true.

Exactly correct. And at one point several days that is several minutes ago, didn't you mention a photograph or a painting, something hanging on the wall?

Her red hair, necklace of pearl and green dress.

Necklace of coral.

Necklace of coral, exactly correct . . .

. . . hanging on the wall opposite the bed.

Opposite the bed, yes. How can I describe it to our listeners. She is gazing out of the frame to her right or the viewer's left. Her expression is serious though not severe. What else?

Her arms . . .

. . . her arms hang at her sides. No—her left arm . . . her left arm . . .

She's sitting at a desk.

At her desk, yes, the desk is to the left of the door as you enter and the bed to the right. I'd forgotten the desk, where was I?

In a room overlooking a river and hills beyond covered with olive trees. And I?

On an ocean voyage.

An ocean voyage, yes, I have been travelling, my head in a kind of brace or cage, the surface calm, the light . . .

. . . very flat, so that it seems to open inward, this blueness if I may call it that, buildings empty, hills almost liquid if there *were* hills. You spoke of a white ship, a 'cruising yawl' as I remember.

26

Yes, I have a description right here:

> "Seen from the air this region of rivers winding their way through flat country presents a pattern of arcs and meanderings of stagnant water. The river-bed itself seems to be edged with pale curves, as if nature had hesitated before giving the river its present, temporary course. At ground level, the Pantanal becomes a dream landscape, where herds of zebus take refuge on the tops of hillocks which look like floating arks, while in the flooded swamps flocks of large birds, such as flamingos, egrets and herons, form dense white-and-pink islands, less feathery however than the fan-like foliage of the caranda palms, the leaves of which secrete a precious wax, and whose scattered clumps offer the only interruption in the deceptively smiling vistas of this aquatic desert."

You mean that's your idea of desire, with all those commas?

We lay becalmed for days, the sea wine-red, my head in a kind of brace or vise. I am a woman or man over seven feet tall, emerald green, crossing an endless field or meadow . . .

. . . hills almost liquid if there *were* hills . . .

. . . and the still air and intense heat of midday . . .

. . . forcing us to take shelter in the shade of the great cottonwoods by the river.

Yes, *perfect*, 'the great cottonwoods by the river.'

And to complete the picture a vast, cobbled public square dating from Roman times, an arcaded town hall decorated with frescoes, and a web of narrow streets filled with couples walking arm in arm. I am sitting in a cafe on the square, my left hand holding a copy of the Kansas City Star folded in half lengthwise, my right holding a spoon and idly stirring coffee in an oversized cup. And so on. The important spot over the head, irregular on one side, straight on the other, like the stripes of the dress, belongs more to her than to the wall; in balancing the head, this vertical form also helps to measure its tilt and the waviness of the hair and costume. On the right shoulder at the sleeve, the odd little puff continues the movement of the hair and accents the inclination of the head. The bands of the dress contribute a soft, wavering current of feeling channeled to the head and prolonged in the silhouette of the hair.

The flame-red hair.

No, dark brown, actually almost black, but I liked that business about the 'smiling vistas of the aquatic desert,' and the 'large flocks of birds.' Thought of using it myself.

Yes, 'the deceptively smiling vistas of this aquatic desert,' and all within the space of a small, sparsely furnished room . . .

. . . overlooking the river. I would usually get up about noon, buy the daily paper and walk to one of the large cafes on the square for coffee and rolls . . .

. . . your face painted blue . . .

. . . and open to desire like a storm or small room, the air always heavy by the river, she raises both arms behind her head to unclasp the coral necklace.

Yes, the sun at its zenith, winged figure with arms extended, and a white ship, exactly correct. Let me tell you what it is you said. The lovers' limbs twist like a river. Their talk is a naming or being named. My back sometimes aches. Their talk hides in the telling. The wind moves us. Wands come and cups, gardens, someone in a cloak, the wind moves us, laws, young girl and the bird at her wrist, colors, bright yellow or blue. I am a woman or man under green sky, garden to my right and then it's the following day. I am a woman or man under emerald sky, wind brushes the river's surface, we talk until our talk becomes hidden.

And when does a play begin?

Don't you remember?

I remember trying to think of who to talk to and what to say. I remember trying to remember what happened on a given day, what word stood for what color, and where we had been and where we had gone. I remember the red studio and the woman in blue, and I remember the one who swallowed his tongue.

Do you remember all the listening?

28

I remember wandering completely lost and looking for the river. I remember hills and gilded domes . . .

. . . narrow streets between high buildings . . .

. . . narrow streets between high buildings . . .

. . . and the lists of irregular verbs . . .

. . . lists of irregular verbs.

To be is to be seen.

To be is to be seen.

Talk is a naming.

Talk is a naming or a being named . . .

. . . and desire an electric shade of blue . . .

. . . electric shade of blue.

Lovely weather today.

Lovely weather, clear and cold . . .

. . . with emerald sky . . .

. . . under emerald sky, rosemary and hyssop in bloom—uh—in bloom—uh—some marigolds—right, marigolds—clouds—probably clouds—things with—uh—names scattered about—uh—and so on————just 'and so on.'

So *you're* the one who swallowed his tongue!

Now I remember—the play *has* begun!

Idem 2

(for more than two voices)

Rebeginning and beginnings is what she told me or what she showed me, cup raised carefully to lip, *etwas gänzlich neues zu lernen*, cover each page completely and waste no space.

Papa breathes in a great eyeful.

Leaves falling and I can hear each one as it touches the water.

Beginning and rebeginning to fall, and I can hear the water.

    (bell rings)

A great eyeful, quiet as a mouse.

A large bucket full of water.

A bucketful and waterfall and a forest.

A voyage.

Seven words learned in winter.

Such as ice to walk on.

Such as Dogtown Common.

    (bell rings)

(pitch pipe: slurred F#—F—E, repeated a few times)

F# to E means a winter voyage.

A ship crossing water and a father.

And an icy passage.

But does he have to play while we're trying to talk?

I'm sorry, what?

(pitch pipe: F# with a lot of vibrato, held for a long breath)

A father?

I'm sorry, what?

(pitch pipe: A, with even more exaggerated vibrato, held as long as possible, i.e. until breath is exhausted)

That's better but not . . . but not . . .

(exasperated) . . . but not *what?*

    (bell)

I'm telling you he pissed in his pants when he died.

A great eyeful—something new each time.

I had to clean it all up.

You 'dropped the porcelain cup'?

I had to *clean it all up*!

    (bell)

He tries to breathe his eyes open wide.

A forest calls the boy a child . . .

. . . and breathes a great eyeful . . .

. . . tree and book and book and tree and book . . .

. . . and leaves beginning to fall . . .

. . . and rebeginning to fall . . .

. . . and a sound like water.

Idem 3
(for two voices speaking rapidly and simultaneously)

Tree and book and book and tree and book. Music we refuse to forget. A voyage. A pair of them talk, swallowing hard, then part. She accompanies snow, observes the water in its course, a pair of us talk. She accompanies them both, tries to walk from 'A' to 'B' knee-deep in snow and ends up lost. We listened to music through the winter over there Mozart but over here Corelli and Bach, over there Landini but here Couperin and Rameau. And I talk in my voice because it's warm, because it's warm and faces north. He talks in her voice because he must: Ruby My Dear, Little Rootie Tootie, Pannonica; I Surrender Dear, There's Danger in Your Eyes Cherie, April in Paris; In My Solitude, I'm Getting Sentimental over You, Everything Happens to Me; I Should Care, Remember, Memories of You. He corners her voice in blue light with plain white border, is that you Harry, George I think there's someone at the door, careful with that package Mr. Kupcak it's filled with extremely delicate spiders. New York and London winter and quarter-inch Tuscan winter, faces a lithium blue, eyes never still, pause for breath here then continue at the designated pace. Her voice entered in the shape of a woman's body, music emanating from the left hand, green velvet gown reaching the floor and trailing behind her as she walked. Then another card, dog and wolf baying at the moon, twin towers, the river, and another, Three of Pentacles reversed, mediocrity and weakness, and finally the Six of Swords, a journey by water. Music we remember to forget, and the room itself, bed to the right as you enter, wood-burning stove in far left-hand corner to one side of the window, washstand with mirror and porcelain pitcher and bowl to the other. Thought of it as the language room, entirely nouns, a head-ache that lasted six days, numbness down the left side, lovely curl of smoke. Lights of the fishing boats and of the cars and trucks on the cliff road. Light pouring from the palm of her left hand. He would sit for hours in an apparent daze at one of the tables hidden from the street. Beginnings are what she showed me, scent of thyme and mint in the July air, the Fool a zero holding a white rose. For years he would wake trembling at four in the morning thinking he had heard a scream.

Idem 4
(for one voice)

look I have been had entered a room large or small had entered have been they wondered a door

hills I remember

hills I remember hills white walls at first light lines of red across the snow

look he said I have been

winter like straw bright domes gilded domes narrow halls eight of wands great hope

look she said I am entering

winter a seamless wall winter bent double each word misspoken red dress coral necklace one or two things have been said

and now I say yes

now I say yes to the bridge the dead cross no thicker than a fingernail no wider than a knife eyes fixed on the Gates of Paradise yes to the visible hills the actual hills olive trees with grey underleaf commas between each breath brief tremor smell of gunpowder then screams it was screams and screams all the way through

idem the same same hills same trees I remember a door

and one wonders I wondered one wonders what direction and remembers why did they have you ever when he said oh well and remembers was burning with what question what direction oh well had almost I'm turning what star then winter had they been even though falling backward of them would discuss from her dream had been had been worrying isn't yet are coming either hand and remembers oh well oh no don't ever saw nothing fell from means winter fell toward means winter fell into felt nothing is empty she believes me what question then winter had told him we're arriving then opened meaning bridges oh well meaning bridges oh well meaning rivers

and the air perfectly calm sky red yellow or blue streets filled with no one she loved the winter loved to lie for hours in the midnight sun left arm crooked beneath her head the right at her side idem the same is then plus now

so slept through seasons of heat and cold and one of rain fell from a high window she wandered into the hills beyond the river never to be seen again slight rustling of the leaves lilac in flower bed of white poppies he woke inside her dream listen he said how can I said she

as there is no image no city no image no one speaking he would lie the entire day eyes focussed on the ceiling turns toward the wall pen in her left hand small notebook in her right light snow coating the balcony trickle of blood from his thumb sky red yellow or blue grey if rain fell forward bruising her temple cupped palm holding three brilliant stones woke wondering again who she was

and there is as there is no image no city horizon four swords no image a circle tall grass a field from a window river from a field no image no city cold rain seven stars then we slept no image pitched forward toward the water fell over in the doorway light snow against a wall bright stones in her palm no image no city no images to come

Music Rewritten

(after D.S.)

Yes and no then yes and no
Soon there'll be time enough for you

Charlie has swallowed the fluid
L has come inside a box

which some people paid to watch
Yes and no yes and no

You are a damaged set of illustrations
You are a ladder

in a chemical pond
a piece of hurry-up cake

or a true-to-life machine
making a music judged incomplete

by everyone willing to speak
Yes and no and yes and no

In a strange country you feel at home
because the hills there are the opposite of green

exactly as you were told
Now you must go there to prove it's so

Yes and no yes and no
Soon there'll be no time for you

The words are lost in the crease
but order is found at the base of a statue

or better, at the foot of a curved stone wall
in the tangles of the grass

Beneath the shadow of no and yes
nothing can be said

First there's sameness then difference
then the letter X across a face

then a line through a name
which is the wrong name in any case

The Village of Reason

This is a glove
or a book from a book club

This is the sun
or a layer of mud

This is Monday,
this an altered word

This is the village of reason
and this an eye torn out

This is the father
or a number on a chart

This is a substitute,
this the thing you are

This is the varnished picture
or else an accepted response

This is the door
and this the word for door

This is a reflex caused by falling
and this a prisoner with an orange

This is a name you know
and this is the poison to make you well

This is the mechanism
and this the shadow of a bridge

This is a curve
and this its thirst

This is Monday,
this her damaged word

This is the trace
and this the term unmarked

This is the sonnet
and this its burning house

You are in this play
You are its landscape

This is an assumption
the length of an arm

This is a poppy,
this an epilogue

Symmetrical Poem

There is interest in being able to feel what you see
an unparalleled achievement of the imagination
even in January, and then to fall back
from the effect of an ancient tent
or text called the Suburban Blend

onto a patterned carpet. So paper
is made from stone and stone from solid
air we call glass, wavy ridges photographed
on sand beaches, thin sheets
marking each dune. The warriors, fearing God,

practice here and the readers
read and are read here, desiring
to be soldiers as well. Do not
look up you may think to tell them
but the words will fail to come out.

The Painted Cup

This was not experience
but life itself and the hills
not visible an iron
table set among the blues. Un-
acknowledged years will have passed
across their faces, so the long-billed
ibis, cautiously
to take bread at your hand
like the infant named
for the one who laughs and,
laughing, fills the painted cup
with coarse salt. The angled
areas between them then, cast
in a range of hues
that to speech are as distant,
or dissonant, matter.

I was talking to the Baroness

I was talking to the Baroness in the Green Room
  The page detached, flew away
toward the northwest
  skimming the still surface
New York was wonderful in those days
  like an island but smaller
though the headlines were awful
  face turned to the wall
the shapes empty colours and forms
  breakwater, mulberry, sign
of the flower opening, sign
  of the flower crystallized
I'm often in London
  less than half alive
Who are the letters A
  Who is Baraka
Sterling Brown in the blue car
  Elmo, Bud, James P.
Nancy and Sluggo
  Axel Hugo Teodor Theorell
to adjust the mirror
  so that the head disappears
who la danseuse magnétique
  qui se mettra d'elle-même en mouvement
sur une table lisse
  Then one must close the mouth quickly
and clench the teeth
  fearing pious old men
all those things that take time
  a maxim handed down to us
between sleeps
  fluid and secret charm

as the z of xylophone
      What fame! What a century
of empty skies, anodynes,
      moving sidewalks
Wet snow is falling once more
      The scene as always is tropical

Sign

Are you asleep M. Valdemar
The survival is untenable
an impossibility of dying
the way smoke rises and comes to rest
overhead, about the light—
that impulse to tell you intimate things
among the floats in a foreign place
projecting oneself into the details
the *a* of anvil for example, anterior,
atopia, at the particular, unstable moment

How install violence, pleasure, irony
and so on as apparent finalities
fragmented into a practice which
erases science, then into words
the opposite of names. So the five
of fingers could become *eyes*,
effort, *these*, *air*, *dust*, where
to another it might mean *flowers*,
a verb whose subject marks years
As for eyes

they are healing, the redness
and pain diminishing each day
Soon the stolen shadow reappears,
the vine on the grey lattice trembles,
the china folk fall from the china wall
An ant is an ideal reader
and there are so many of them
Sad Electra emerges from the forest
and approaches the shore
The conversation, long deferred, begins

easily sometimes, sometimes not at all,
a story whose end I know
and don't know, airs
against the summer's dust
these, head in such an effort
of turning as to resemble
world, "a certain sacrifice"
for the meadow orchids, ospreys,
rugosas and wild currants
Time is passed in saying nothing

by telling things. The chimneys
are not real
but after-images from the dream,
what remained of the houses
in the mountain village
The teacher was the goat-herd's lover
Lightning struck the iron bed,
something to remember in a storm
I do not face the world, I face the wall
Could you be here for that week

Language paralyzes the tongue
and before morning the father is gone
I was born with no right hand
below the street of diamonds
in a city of constant groans
Experience cannot be described
except by us. We
fled down the marble steps
We spoke the prime sentence and dissolved
Everything of smoke was ours

Left Unfinished Sixteen Times

I is the director of three letters and the dead director.

And I is the reader's "not yet" within the letter.

I includes the one incapable of mentioning death in the event, or else the director or else the dead letter.

(This could be said not to be written.)

I is enclosed by the question where it's read as a letter.

I might pretend to be a reading in the letter, its circuit diagram or "music hall full of fun" or weighing of symptoms and costs.

I refers to the pause or loss, the decision that a window will remain closed the better to watch.

I thought it would be nice to make some chemicals, to make some lexical adventures to enlarge the space, then reside forever in the silence of the letter.

I is directed by the names of three letters, unnaming the dead director.

And I is the reader's forgotten letter.

Where I is mentioned there is a pause or loss, a papered hall lit at intervals by backward letters.

Where I goes unmentioned there exists an alternate version filled with cups, diagrams, quills and jars.

Perhaps a farm beneath the sea.

This omits, perhaps deliberately, the question of the head and neck, position of the hands, and the rope between her teeth drawn slowly across the floor.

It omits or forgets who they are and who the others are who watch.

Then it forgets the words for this and not-this, for first and for again.

Then imitating I he says, "Forgetfulness must be remembered when you insist 'I cannot remember.' " Who is it will admit to this.

Echo

(texte antiparallèle pour Pascal Quignard)

which resounds. Re-sounds. Where first
would follow. The letter he had lost reap-
peared in his palm. Identity was the cause.
Not that the word spoken had been heard.
Not that a word spoken can be seen, even par-
tially, traced against the screen. Language
copies him in its listening, tracing his imper-
fect copy. Which re-sounds. Echoes briefly.
The rustling a wall transmits by interference.
For example: raised both arms above his
head. And said: a letter a letter can be reck-
oned with. Rustling as of an article of cloth-
ing such as a dress or green dress. An even
greyness as of a page, recording events. The
subject is this, rustling at the moment of
enunciation, to be reckoned with. Not that
the words thus raised above the head and
turned into hills. Could possibly. Be recog-
nised in his own misunderstanding. After the
talking is done a kind of attention to each
mark, an injured identity traced against the
screen. Soweto-Miami. Cremated beside the
river.

which sounds (sounded) different at night.
Not that the words reassembled among hills,
exactly, where there were none. A rustling
seized him, the history of cloth and wind,
hedgerows. Or windows above rivers, corn-
flowers and forget-me-nots, an even blue-
ness as of a page, a failure at translation. The
distant past visited and we whispered her

well. Heard prior to itself and dressed as a
shadow. Not that the words resembled hills
exactly, hidden among them. Soweto-
Miami as of a particular light, a quality. Hills
where there were none, only sounds. Body
of perhaps a dog, afloat, the first ten notes,
major then the minor mode. Echoes an atten-
tion.

as if preceding, preceded by, itself, depth of
the forest. The subject is this, disregarded,
story of cloth and wind or the space between
events.

misunderstood as a measure of distance. It
takes no time in that sense, repeats nothing,
figures the shape of the flames. Gesticulate.

a failure of translation. In sleep the language
he spoke was one he didn't know. Waking it
sounded the same. Waiting there it seemed a
succession of names, a level field of things in
constant motion, exchanging identities.

neither followed nor following. Two are
there as she counts to one, to one and one then
three five eight defining the spiral, to double
sevens to begin, to instauredness. Left arm
and right and the figures like the fire. There
must be a different metric, a gesture and that's
all, this this and so on, concomitance, like
writing but it's not a writing, the pieces ac-
tually are.

across water. Soweto-Miami with no dis-
tance, the figures the fragments of a picture.
She refused the explanation before it was
made. Who (previous to speaking) woke

against a door. Right arm detached these past weeks, greyness modified at each stage.

This I saw and said at once.

Case where he has visions of his dead friend.

in gesturing there. The letter he had lost was the cause, an imperfect copy spoken among hills or reassembled there.

The letter he had lost was the cause, a dead friend traced against the screen. They are listening to songs while waiting for morning.

Forgetting the name as it sounds, an unknown city, the journey never begun. Letter (book) deafened by echoes, figure (form), an even greyness indicating the river.

What we call depth then, of forest, mirror, conviction etc., voiced as fake history. As morning is said to offer new hope or no hope in what must be or may have been a courtyard where photographs substitute for trees, benches and walls, each detail perfectly reproduced from the story he was told about how it all would eventually appear. Thus the severed head is an object of polite discussion and necessary to the tableau like the polychrome statuary and exotic flora we admire more than words can say.

She claims they are trying to fuck their way into history and so to change it, and for a moment we both do and do not agree. The river in the background is muddy, the lamenting figures the same shape as the flames. The subject, disregarded, is the frequency of the oscillation, the coincidence of cloth and wind, hedgerows. She discovered the pen beneath her bed.

of interest because unspoken: to the eye over water; softly repeated; erasure in the naming; 'many-tongued.'

She discovered the pen and returned it to him.

disappeared then, leaving a voice behind unlike her own.

They do both agree and disagree, the numbers and voices projecting above the ostinato figure, violinist the father's son, lawns crisp and green, indifferent, the visible world, auricle of the ear cool, fresh, rough, succulent to the touch.

She claims they want to agree but disappear while speaking, brief redness of history softly repeated, the severed head a substitute for trees intended as an aid to memory.

She claims they want to eliminate history, legs turned to smoke, carriage passing a row of columns said to be endless because it does end.

A very narrow but not very tall glass-domed house with two entrances. Nodded as if she believed what I'd said, carriage rocking on its worn springs, a constant trembling.

So it is equivocal and precedes its beginning.

I over there, he-she here, table and lamp.

is brought forward from, toward the eye. Water's moment as of blocks, uninvited, a one-hinged sound that sleep recited, what he was of, half-yellowed now by leaves, as of blocks carved clumsily and set afloat, stairs cast in darkness, curtain held tightly shut then drawn a little apart, a redness to history reflected wherever words might turn to talk and tell of a mirrored door.

which to be so must remain closed?

and so and so. He told her what she'd once told him.

Dear Janet, When I want to get away from it all I pick up one of your novels and—presto—mission accomplished!

Whether dreaming is thinking about something. Whether the eyelids moving are seeing.

which to be so must remain closed?

naked to waist with back turned, arms enfolding head, world large by lamplight rolling us even in sleep, a redness to the story they'd been told.

He painted her beside herself as a likeness, and each face seemed identical with the one they had known.

She claims they are trying to erase the story by repeating it exactly as it was told. Thus clematis, tea, rhubarb, Indian fig, water and its cognates, of worlds twice seven, wheat and corn. Thus table and lamp (or desk and light), sheets (or leaves), wordless talk, gestural dreams empty of meaning, palms in para-muthetic wind. This with my own words she told him.

And told him again.

Echo

(alternate text)

The two poles. We didn't disagree
that meetings should be begun

upon our foreheads—slender
memories had been put to death

in the proper style, encounters
with forests, mountains

and fields, creatures returning
from islanded sleep

said nothing
nervous and unattended

as we wept. This habit of yellow paper
is recent and without effect

upon our foreheads—slender
runners outstripped them

and said nothing
as we wept. What

time of day now
might say differently

'this weapon is invisible,' or
this name so pronounced

with lips inconceivably apart
has been lost

within its sound,
might then among the *llaneros*

recite tales of night rides
that take no time

or nothing if not time
to tell. Visitors gathered there to hear

it said—backward
it's true—that

he and she were
this and this, not

any one shade exactly
not any one thing

outlined by its clarity
against the milky glass.

At a given moment lovers pass
in complicated hats

the wind will later take back.
The bedstead is iron, with-

out ornament and not mine. Its
fading is what recalls it

to them, an imaging of the rings
of fractured ice

coating volute and column
overhead. Yet some of those

paths were like maps, green
for no reason, pale

orange where no one had been.
Knowledge is empty claimed the swaying bridge.

She recognised the voice as her own
resounding in the damp hall

though the rest,
what the words now said

again and again,
seemed entirely different.

Echo

(a commentary)

which in a dry season might
begin or might precede its
beginning with a list
of truths self-evident: these
clouds (these crowds) you
now see are permanent
and fixed; the arboreal splendor, the
meadows and chalk cliffs
are artificial, devised
of wired concrete and paint
by a developer in the forties
and therefore beautiful; he took
three breaths for every one of hers;
the sun's chariot hurried backward
in its path to a point
exactly overhead and two months before;
the child had trouble speaking;
war was once again in the air;
the space program was to blame for the
snow; nervous
brides waved
weapons in the air; passions
and sensations succeed each other; I
stumbled; I recognised Bugs Bunny;
the darker one had not yet
closed her eyes; weight of a mass
of fair hair; below
a certain temperature the pen
would not write; below
them lay a square
filled with soldiers and statues;
the road north from the city

parallels the river; some
laughed and turned their backs;
enclosed were seven songs;
the letters grew bolder;
heat, cold, light, shade;
the key broke off in his hand;
they lived beneath the streets
to evade certain death; the name
began with a *L* or possibly an *R*;
he scored the loaf at each day's portion;
the distribution of brightness oscillates;
bells mark points in space;
an odor of sulphur penetrated the room
though the windows had been carefully sealed;
one could see the outline of a movement
there; was I the source of such dreams
without meaning; actual
dancers traced against the ceiling;
a bluish violet; echoes
as of such voices
which once had claimed to be real;
a city then they would later imagine
pendant to the west like a jet bead
except empty; the rose she called *cette*
apparition sanglante, cette image;
the apple falls straight down
injuring thousands; we mounted the scaffold
at his unspoken invitation;
a liquid darkness there;
figures lost among the bands of light
came slowly forward; a duplicate
of herself encountered in passing
nodded and disappeared; it remains
visible above the narrow shore;
they are visible against the shore;
the forgotten word for waves; hazelnut
and monkey-flower; the key first
spoken of; wide azure borders.

Book of the Yellow Castle

This can be seen as placing a mirror against the page.
The mountain is where we live, a circus there, a triangle
of unequal sides the days no sun appears.

This is life in the square inch field of the square foot house,
a September particle, biochip, or liquid in a jar,
and here is snow for the month to follow, light easy to move

but difficult to fix. The cat on the book has fleas.
It's a real cat with real fleas at least,
while the book is neither fixed nor field.

As soon as you had gone an image formed in order to be erased.
First an entryway then a left and right which seemed to be the same.
This letter explains everything and must never be sent.

This other arranges figures along an endless colonnade
imperceptibly darkening toward red. One pretends to be the case
the other is. Mornings the hands tremble, evidence of a missing thought.

Arrows will tell you where the words are meant to lead,
from hall to hall apparently. The hair is thinner
and the veins stand out a bit more.

Who could have known he'd be dead within the week,
victim of a loosening thread, the system by which we perceive.
Thus the castle above valley and plain, the logical circuitry and other such tricks,

the constant scanning, all kinds of features built in.
And thus the difference between sign and sigh, and the bells which signal a return.
The dog instructs the goats, the man instructs the dog.

Should we count the remaining trees to decide what they mean as well,
traces of a conversation possibly, or a larger plan. You enter the stories as a surd
and sleep through them, ignoring successive warnings,

shards of cloisonné, broken table legs, a canopied bed.
They are there because the rest have left.
These are scalings of a sentence.

Multiples

for A.S.

Well the hearts are—is—
where you find 'em
The coffee spilled
all over the table
a calculus of variations

in itself
bears no requirement
as to number, form
This error we insist on
as we insist on

torn pockets, one
to each hip
causing us to walk
somewhat differently
than before

Fractal Song

for C.G.

I do not know where I will be in July
Sam said or said Sam

The sound so measured has no boundary,
is not triangle or square

We pass through it in false flight, relieved
to be there, to be hearing

once again at least
the tick of the cup at the Clarion

Clouds are not spheres we know
now, and mountains not cones

Musica Ficta

This I will never tell. I slept under a thing. It was a feather. Then the envelope slipped. I will tell you about this. We are not listening. We are gradually and of necessity enveloped. We are victims of the feather and this is telling.

I will speak of this. You are the listener in memory. You are the thing that seems missing, possibly forever. We are in a room speaking but not listening. There is no room for listening. I hear a car, then a tree. I'm in a city.

I'm in a city in a room that seems missing. I will speak of this in a way that's telling. My love was a feather, etc. In memory we are emptied, are there for the telling. We are the means of telling things, of telling things that are missing. I will say nothing of this. I will say it to anyone listening. I slept under a tree.

I will tell you a story. The cat drank from the glass meant for me. Sleep is this in a way, a thing like a story with the hands sawed off. No one has work and no one cares. We are enveloped, etc. The car passes a tree. We are enveloped, etc.

I will tell you a little tale. The smoke enveloped me, staining the weave and altering the fabric of things. We spoke with a certain elegance, like glass, melting only gradually. It is true that sand is made of glass. This is its identity without question. Why else would we lie there. I repeat. Why else, etc.

Some things are empty as they are meant to be. Not the world or its clumsy replica. Not therefore or anyway. Not the sad-eyed Jew running fingers through his hair. Not the hand itself or its embarrassing tremor. Not the sentence or its clumsy replica. Now everything can really begin. Now we will pretend all songs are possible.

You are not unlike a bell. These excerpts. The why of history. The photograph of history. This mask for this journey, as it's said, with a transparent gesture. Of this once again or this never. A kind of economy. An acknowledgment.

The music's idea is this. We are in a room thinking but not speaking. A tree has damaged a car. We are gradually enveloped. We must say nothing of this. It is a reference, a sort of numbered set, too little of too much. A city made of sand made of glass. Or a measured distance for which the octave stands.

First Figure

for Ben Watkins

The name is spelled without letters how can this be. There are no steps leading to this house, no objects anymore. I have some questions do I not. The reactor has been wounded, that willow perfect, a swimmer not entirely of the world. Humble yourself before the workers. Die eagerly in battle. The water music now unweighted. The terrified child pretends not to hear. Its lions as the library burns. This signals my end. One thing the beloved another the blood. The smoke returns. The hands of the acrobats connect. The name plummets. The eye carves a path. The "A" of "Not A." The attraction to another felt as cork or ink. Calendar etched in wall. The "A" as "Not A." The woman reading, woman sleeping. The view from the studio, Cour de Rohan. The landscape with chestnuts, landscape with goats. The nude resting. The rose of close observation. The smoke as mine returning. The words altered then crossed out. Returning that is into the body. A refusal of the particular body. "I am not somebody here," as spoken by the servant. The medicine on the sill and the light through it. Another light said to be revealing, a third termed awkward. A story in the form of a question to be answered by another in the form of a question and so on. May I speak to Muriel. So much through that door. Myself as Puddin' 'n Pie. The hotel of our crystal delights. Now your turn while the numbers last. Now ours not theirs.

What might be said before the sentences enter: there is no focal point; I have no idea what the future will bring; we did not make the new law ourselves.

The name is felt without letters how can this be. The cat then the ghost of the cat continually reappearing. A reading of an evening. Here the first figure, here the false figure of speech playing with a ring. Here once more the coffee and the moth, damp bread in hunks, habits of afterwards and opposite. There are no steps leading to this. Not ours not theirs. A city of domes soon to be torn down. A sad monkey-house or the five random letters for the fingers of the hand. The story you've been looking for may well lie there. She steps from the shower and reaches for a towel. The story may well lie there in a cloud. Everyone knows these things by heart. Everyone tells these things from the heart.

64

The word is all that is displaced. This illness I stole from my father. A love of figures, tidiness, fear of error. These are the new remains. She shifted her position almost imperceptibly. He was reluctant to agree at first. They might have it otherwise, simpler perhaps, no columns in the space. They might care to see it in another light, simpler perhaps, deducting shadow. The field itself is yellow, with the usual points of reference. Then evening with its blue coat, perfume jars, obstacles, machines held onto. It was quite a short pleasure. The police know all about it.

Ab Urbe Condita

Call it the first distinction
the mark of a mark

a book named "laws" or "Magee"
"rude logic" or "noble lady"

and its magic version
with the houses at the foot of the tower

and the clock-hands pointed toward white
The man is seen from behind walking away

holding a baguette of freshly baked bread
the same dog at his heels

and there might be a dazzled moth or profile
or so-called arabesque of trees

each considered more than real
A decaying staircase leads to the first floor

It will break once you step on it
Moving vans waited where the gardens had been

I'm writing simply about the wind, the
wind and the cat, the cat and the mirror, the child's

chair with broken back
says he. These would be the last nights

that had just been painted around the walls
The man can be seen swallowing a frog

This Time

(another for Sarah)

Once I fell in the ocean when
I didn't know I fell in the ocean

Then Momma got me out
This isn't true

only something I remember
Once in the park I broke in half

and lost one half
which half I don't remember

Once I was in a room
It grew larger and larger

why I don't remember
One time I turned blue all over

then got clear as glass
This really happened

but not to me
Once I couldn't see

for a while
so I listened lying down

Another time I looked out the window
and saw myself at the window

across the street
This time it was me

Six Illustrations

1. LITTLE FIRES
From the balcony we see a town we see a lake we see walkers along the shore
beyond the rail. We see through the green chair and we see little fires
instead of faces and the trunk of a tree interrupted by lines
crossing at what would have been an horizon
to the figure asleep and the watching child

2. CARLUCCIO
From the singing mouth the thread plays out

3. ATLANTIC WINDOW
They are lovers aligned by blue
Her hands have disappeared into him
and so she might speak of wakes and flares
meaning wakes of scanning eyes
and flares on the surface of the lake

4. THE QUESTION (Semitic Garden)
Do you not know yet
how lightly they rest

5. SCENE INCLUDING (Joseph's House)
The house arrives then the house arrives
Each is placed in a line

Each one is a house
Each house is of a size to be held in two hands

Sometimes the hands will gesture back and forth
then form a bridge with no one on it

6. THE QUESTION (Semitic Garden)
Sometimes they will murder each other
then go to sleep

Sometimes they will murder each other
in order to sleep

There is a reason for this
which they will forget

τροπή

The altered body
in parts or particles

by the sun-clock
The train passes, the last

until tomorrow
I will not ask

before entering
as I once did

The ink makes a sound
The cranes are asleep

and this is how they look
The book had some pages

Wet it becomes a brick
to play with then discard

As a Real House

(Sarah's third song)

"I said darkling and you said sparkling"
The play-house appears before us

as a real house in the dark
filled with people cut out

of magazines and postcards
and called real people at the start

Why is the curtain partly drawn
and why does the stair turn

to the left as you climb
and the right going down

Here all day it's midwinter night
and the musicians will continue to play

in the music room
and sleep will never come

This is lesson three
where the fiddler is made real

by the sound she hears
pouring from her fingers

Facades for Norma Cole

These ornaments as we pass
to which thin lines are attached
the straight dark hair, bordered

hollows and lights, double spirals
imagined weights of things
If only I could draw, then

there would be an owl here
a fox in the elm's shadow
Bill do you remember the Chinese man in the stained grey overcoat

lying dead on the snow
by the brick wall
A remarkable document

which must never be published
He turned round to answer
but she was gone

then ran through the streets before passing out
on the steps of a synagogue
the face no longer recognisable

even to my closest friends
These crystals, however
Or put it this way

the particles circle and circle inside the ring
all the while accelerating
until finally by the billions they collide

That's how the missing one was found
Let's call it W for now
which fuels the stars

and so add one more line
extending from the woman with naked breasts
at the center of the arch

to the cat asleep on the child's bed
They spoke of exactly this over coffee
until the glass door shattered

letting the damp wind enter
In her room she showed me
a photograph of her lover

young, heavily muscled and tanned
from several months at sea
We drank wine, smoked

opium through a glass pipe
and climbed to a place on the ridge
a field of nettles and anise

where the remains of the city could be seen
not this city but a previous one
called the pissing rose

or the rhymesters' rose
or the rose of even numbers
or the rose of indecision

or the rose of precise description
or *la rose dialectique, Dominique*
all yours again

in tenuous modes of oscillation
'neath a vestigial sky
"Look—there was a wall here once"

No one did this
It came about by itself
during yesterday's storm

A Souvenir of Japan

There are shadow figures for a new world
but I have no question to ask you.
The watery gates
have already told everything
needing to be known
and the sentence is there
free at last to occur
in some other direction

(or the fiery gates, whichever
you prefer). So many drawn
to the one narrow enclosure
and none ever emerging
or so at times it seems.
Maybe none even want to
knowing that on the other side
they will only find more stairs

and more doorways to turn from.
Each day in this forest is like the last
as her notebook indicates.
Odd that it contains no words
just stories and the remains
of a few interarboreal
insects pressed
by chance between the pages.

Yet she never used words, never
knew any, so why
should we have expected them
suddenly to appear. Do you remember this
and do you admit to it.

Steam rose from the lantern
lighting that place
unless it had been a name

but not a place.
I will always carry the beads
in case the subject of truth
and beauty does come up.
Their dominant colors seem to be
pyroprene with psychomachia,
winding path, arrow and circle,
the end was extremely near.

A kind of gauge-field is required
to restore invariance
a bracketed logic
between field and gaze.
This is simpler than it sounds.
The heart is monitored
causing a riddling mark across the screen
yielding non-random information

there for anyone to read.
New angles will be added
as it grows. The columns
are encrusted with paint
various whites most recently
and below these a muddy green. What
costume in fact to wear
for what occasion. She has returned

and I've spoken with her.
She resembles herself in nothing else
but this single thing
and that may well be enough,
the four layered voices and leading tones
over the measured shuffling of feet.
The patterns in such a space
would repeat and repeat.

Of this cloth doll which

(Sarah's fourth)

Of this cloth doll which
says Oh yes
and then its face changes
to Once upon a time
to Wooden but alive
to Like the real
to Late into the night
to There lived an old
to Running across ice
(but shadows followed)
to Finally it sneezed
to The boat tipped over
to Flesh and blood
to Out of the whale's mouth

Yes in a circle

(Sarah's fifth)

Yes in a circle the imagined train
word after recent word
you make them up to come to mean
light to shadow day
pond as music's mirror
trees cut from yarrow stalks
would be real in order to seem
a reasonably green place
a reasonable number of roads
some straight, some curved and narrow
beside rails whose perfect parallels
are nowhere else to be seen
but in a sealed and measured space
called here and now for now

View from an Apartment

The word "dream" is technical and means nothing
so we can use it
whenever we want
Max's dream has masks
and is lit from the side and the back
I did not dream this dream
but lay with eyes open instead
and the dancers were my friends
We have lived a life that lasted some time
Now we live another, liquid one
Our vestments are invisible
say the crows
Our lake is a secret
imperfectly kept
says the Ténébreuse
You must stay awake until this ends

Design by David Bullen
Typeset in Mergenthaler Bembo
by Wilsted & Taylor
Printed by McNaughton & Gunn
on acid-free paper